MW01602786

AMERICAN DREAM

Emelda Suh

ISBN: 978-1-4834-5552-5 (sc)
ISBN: 978-1-4834-5708-6 (hc)
ISBN: 978-1-4834-5551-8 (e)

Library of Congress Control Number: 2016911938

Lulu Publishing Services rev. date: 08/11/2016

A Strange Land Called America

That means we will have to leave our homes behind and travel by air, sea, or land to this strange land far, far away.

I will stamp my feet and brace for impact, and I will run for the hills.

When the volcanoes from the belly of the mountains roar with hunger, I will fall back to earth, and on my way down, be majestically represented by the eagle.

Let me conquer fear and rise with the wolf, for he alone has seen the world in different shades.

I pray for morning to come so I can see the glorious rise of the sun, thus enjoying the fruitful harvest of the day.

Let me grow in the belly of America and be another American Dream.

My claws have been sharpened by the eagle. My pride rode waves of mountains to make it unbroken.

Humility has been forged into my soul, leaving my ethical sense with a touch of pleasantness, and I refuse to mark time; I want time to mark me.

This talk about the Promised Land of opportunity has my wings flapping toward the sun just in time to catch the wonderful glimpse of the morning light for a brighter tomorrow. I shall remember to buy me a tree and sink my roots deep to the bottom of the ground, for my walk was long and tiresome. I shall now lay my thoughts to rest, because I see through the eyes of a growing America.

My Love for You

I t cannot be spoken of 'cause I will choke.
You looked so lovely today. If I had missed you, I swear it would have stopped a thousand stars from being born. Today I speak not of my love, 'cause it causes my very heart to ache for replacement. Such a close fondness I have found with your name that I make every excuse to hear it.

Yes, a thousand lands were crossed in order for me to tell you this, and a thousand more I am prepared to go over for the sake of my heart problems. A thousand stitches could not keep it from bleeding if you left.

The nights are so cold and lonely, but the thought of you gives me hope, for every echo from your lips makes my eyes linger over the sound effect of the gone words.

Do you care like I care?

Sh, don't answer, my love. Let my hand and my feet move to the sway of the right now, because life is a motion picture, and we must look our best in every scene.

Every glance of you and every gesture drives me insane with desire. Your curves were put together only by the holy unison of love, and your name was picked by matrons before you.

Let me proclaim my love for you like no other before me, because mine is true and yours to keep.

Jungle Lord

Into the deep jungle, with only my backpack and some great boots to keep me warm and a blade for my path, I tread up and down, up and down. The roads look windy and endless, but I look forward to my first jungle meal, which hangs from branches or may come from the pit of an herbivore. Nevertheless, I scan and scan myself to safety. If only there were one in these open—yet so enclosed— cold quarters. The heavens seem so distant.

My itch is real; the bugs do bite, and the snakes are vicious. The hot smell mixed with all the anxiety is giving my belly reasons to churn. I refuse to smell my own pits; a change of shirt will be nice. But away! I must keep moving before the day's lights are swallowed out of me, for the leaves will be way safer when the owls become wide awake.

The days are long and wet; the nights are cold and dreary. My legs go limp with every tread, while my body slowly gives in to its element. In my strong need for a shower, a quick dive into an ocean would be nice. I am not yet hallucinating, for I am only two days into the jungle, and I am describing from a freshman point of view.

Down, down, down, I go, clearing the path as if preparing for a new light or a new beginning to find there is just more to clear out. I am lost in thoughts, and my jungle is now my life as we ascend and descend the slopes of what we call life. One thing is for sure: we cannot predict the future. So why am I clearing? It may be dangerous ahead, but yet away I clear. It must be the adrenaline or the curiosity that keeps me clearing, but one thing is certain: the path looks better from here. Why stop?

No, no, no, no, no. Quitting is not in my DNA. My doctor has never prescribed failure. Defeat is just another six-letter word. My patience will pay off. I shall reap my benefits tomorrow—not today, not today. I shall grow strong mentally and physically to complete the task ahead. I will peruse the jungle well enough to become a jungle lord, for then will I be worthy to sing with the birds, echo my own echo, and cry with the late-night rain.

I have become one with this adventure, giving me a different and keen understanding of the delicateness of the green leaves and the metamorphosis that takes place. This beautiful jungle is waiting for a caress to send her into bloom. I will hate to be her lover and, yes, am not worthy of her love. She is too perfect for a mere human like me, filled with imperfections.

A Mistake in Redding, California

L ife is a stage, and we are all actors on it, playing different roles. Handouts cannot be expected, because no one walks the righteous path. The heavens will fall because hell is black. If I have to survive, I must look to my own script. But what can a man do when his lines seem so blank and blurred? I cannot take another's position 'cause 'tis not mine. My role will be tainted, and I might just mess up everyone else's parts. Or is the role I am supposed to be playing blank and blurred?

Cut! Take three! Action! Whiff! Here we go with this dreaded director, and to think I was just figuring out my script. By the looks of it, 'tis very complicated. But then again, that is the cry of the wild, and I dare not go into the woods, because I will be greeted by the hungry mountain lions. I alone know that would be a mistake in Redding.

Although the faith and kindness of the people will heal my wounds, the scars won't be worth it. I walked ten thousand miles for this role, and nobody will take it from me. My auditions might not go as well, but my faith is unshaken for you who believe still live.

This is my part, and this is my time. I need to search for my black light, for my aquarium light ain't working, and my fish seem not to be moving. I will not dare Photoshop myself in the now to please the crowd; the crowd does very well in keeping itself entertained. Yes, they are here to see me tonight. The stage is mine, and my readings are clean and clear.

For the first time, I look over and notice the director looks tense and unsure. I am calm and confident, and for the first time, I have learned to accept my role and fall in the center stage, right along with others. Today I will not falter. Rather, I will smile broadly and brightly, for that mistake in Redding was a good place to start.

Homeless

The thought of that word and the meaning behind it brings a lot of questions and memories of persecutions. Some might say you are homeless because you made a wrong decision and landed hard on your behind, and you've got nobody to blame but yourself. Others might say you got caught up in the wrong crowd and ended up in a devastating situation and therefore deserve every pinch and punch aimed toward you. Tell people you're homeless, and see the looks on their faces. Why are we humans so judgmental, and why do we fear the unknown? Sure, being homeless ain't all that pretty and glamorous. How can you judge if you have not walked in their shoes? How can you understand the people if you have not interacted with them?

Sure, some are there because of drugs and wrong decisions made, but others are there to put the pieces of their lives together. Does that mean every last one of them is condemned? My eyes have seen, my tongue refuses to roll, but my hand forges on. Sure, there is sadness in the air; the people look to each other for hope, and the jokes they crack are dry and distant. But they still laugh at their own silly mistakes. Their life is one of close community. They care for one another yet steal from one other and betray like no other. Maybe 'tis the curse that comes with the whip.

Hey, no one says it's a perfect world. And if the gloves don't fit, don't wear them. If you are not scared of powered gloves, being cursed out, and getting a little rained on, may I suggest that you stop by, lend a hand, and learn a thing or two along the way.

Don't forget to say hello, because a smile from an outsider and advice from a fresh face might just do some miracles and turn things around, for everyone deserves a second chance. Some do need direction, but again, don't we all? They find themselves lost in translation and look to the old habits for answers, like waiting for manna to fall from the sky. They sin yet they sin no more. They pray for a miracle and hope for an angel to stop at their door, because being homeless sucks.

Hope

When all else fails, hope is what I can count on, the horse I can mount for safety. When all else goes astray, I look upon that word to carry me to safety. I lean on the pillar of hope, for it alone keeps me from sliding in a wrong direction. This rock comforts me in my solace yet forever embraces change. All around me people are full of despair. When I look, I feel I need those four-letter words to lift my head to the sky.

My fingers are grimy, my face is pale, my skin is flush with the hot red liquid that flows through my veins. As I put my hands together, they hug me tight for the days I cannot depend on anyone, because sweet solace can be miserable. Nobody ever said climbing the mountain of hope is easy, for 'tis not the line that is long and dreadful, and not everyone reaches the finish line. But if you do, the harvest is fruitful and one to remember.

What about the fallen? Should they be forgotten and left to feed on the scraps? Should they be redirected onto a smaller mountain because their legs can't take them that far? I refuse to object or subject them to such humiliation, for somewhere in their wounded pride lies hope that no one should take away from them. It leads them to the path of self-reliance that can uplift their spirit. When my wings soar, they are unbroken, for they carry no red spots on them. They are mature and can brave the wind. When I descend for fresh air, no negativity will surround me, because I choose to see the positive impact on others. I do not dwell on their not-so-perfect side, because they believe as I believe. In hope we are all united.

Morning Sunlight

After a long night of sleeping and snoring, I rise to find myself staring at my alarm clock, which will not stop going off. I hit snooze, begging for five more minutes of sleep. What I would give for a couple more hours of sleep! I roll over and catch the morning sunlight; it softly caresses my face, reminding me of a new day. The dreadful thought of the office hours has me pulling my covers over my head. The thoughts of the day begin swirling in my head, as if I need reminding. Worse, I cannot sign off, for the sunlight is giving me new joy for the wish I dared pray for last night.

Nigh, nigh, nigh, my work hours are long, leaving me with little room for romance. Or is that just an excuse to bury my head in work and stay celibate for as long as I can?

I do crave the arms, touch, and feel of a woman but do not miss the gossips, ex-boyfriends, passed-away pets, girlfriends who need redemption, invitations to places I'd rather not go. Thinking of it, this bed feels warmer for some strange reason. I am appreciating my solitude and bonding with my covers, beginning to relax and enjoy the first glimpse of sunlight.

Far, far from emotions I drift as my coffee pot starts to crackle with the sound and smell of fresh roasted beans in the air. Those were imported, and I will drink without being disturbed. I will gulp it down without eyes watching or having to explain why or feel embarrassed that I look a mess this morning. I will savor every drop and let my cheek have some, because this coffee is good. Yes, again I repeat it is imported, for it is that good.

Before I get adorned by the sprinkles of the morning shower or get embellished in the world of fashion and become the center of the attention of my coworkers and offer a yes sir to my boss, I will show myself to the morning sun. For I know you will envy my carelessness. And for this few minutes, I am the boss of me.

A Few Good Men

When I look toward the sun, the rays burn so bright and the light gives me hope. Then again, when I cast my face toward earth, I see a lot I have to work on—we have to work on: the greed of men, the envy of women, the frustrations of the poor, the agony of a grieving mother, and the cries of a newborn that could melt even the hearts of Amazon warriors. I am hopeful there are a few good men left, but I dare not count myself among them, because that will be a lot of ego to give away and yet so little to contribute.

Nay, I bank on morals. If morals don't bank on me, I fetch, because humility pays. Yet I am not a lamb. Though I admire their soft white fur, I am prone to join the hammerhead sharks for a warmer day on the ocean floor. Integrity is so hard to uphold, because as humans we are called to falter—and falter again we shall. But I would like a little piece left, not just a cold turkey. Life is all about principles and what slices we desire. The bigger the bite, the heavier the chew, and the slower it is for the swallow, the searching for that perfect balance instead of a choke. That's confidence all right, mixed with the thoughts of physical health, for only you truly know this as you have sought after temperance.

A few good men will fight for injustice because they are committed, faithful, and actually take the initiative to listen at the same time, being very meticulous with every detail. They push and strive for a better man within while never losing respect for themselves or others. Good men know no racism, because it's only skin deep.

He traveled too far and wide to be bothered by nonsense. He'd rather be the ambassador of peace, the guru of accomplishments, and the speed to lead. His true love of travel and the different spheres he's come across make him more in tune with his surroundings. He will walk a mile in others' shoes but won't fight for a perfect fit, for he knows they are borrowed shoes. He tries them to sense the man he sees.

He believes every new day brings forth another fruitful harvest. He seeks the safest path while taking charge, and not once does he falter in his task, because he knows the price he pays for being in the service of a few good men.

For the Mermaid in Me and the Merman in You

(The Divine Brotherhood of …)

My wet suit is my shield of scales while my board serves as my fins. I am one with the waves and refuse to part with the sweet desire of the ocean. The texts can wait. My friends can adhere to my newfound ego. Things to do, places to see—but all those things suck up my time, for the world can wait. It waited a billion years to see me; it sure can race with me without complaining.

Splash, splash, splash, the sweet dynamite of the waves' call. My blood is on fire; my adrenaline is shooting through the roof. Somebody, please order a paramedic to go, for I can hear the call of the wild, and the battlefield is straight ahead.

My hands are free in the air, like a parachute, for balance. My legs are strapped tight to my superhero board for impact. My eyes are pinned to the ocean for safety's sake. I dare not blink nor think of the great whites, for I can brave any storm because I am part human and live in the ocean part time. That means I've got skin, I've got scales, and I've got sense. Heck, tomorrow I will relax on the boat with my human compatriots, but for now I sleep in the embrace of the blue and let my mirage be painted by the waves of the ocean. For I, among a few others, belong to this trusted brotherhood of …

For the Fallen Veteran Heroes

It's hard to fill that gap. I cannot walk in those shoes; they won't fit, for I refuse to picture the hole that took you away from me. I prefer to remember you as you were: the butt of the barrel, but the first one to stand beside his fellow man, the one to never back down from enemy fire and leave a comrade behind. We were like brothers, some would say, but I like to think we were more than brothers. Some nights together we heard the pained cries from the Dear John letter room or the happy sounds of men chanting for an expecting fellow brother. You have surely served thy country well and fought bravely alongside your brothers. Even though your banner has been burned, your stripes still fly high in my head—in our heads.

The people around me know you or want to know you, for they are helping me through this moment of pain. I need the comfort to relieve me of my hurt. I look to your days of glory and think that if the world had just given you one more day to live, maybe together we would have grown into our old age.

I despise the sadness or anything associated with it, for they don't understand the pain I am going through. I lost a brother I never had and am still learning to cope with it like a man. I know no other way to fade it. Maybe after this somber day filled with grief, I will go back home and pour me a glass of something hard and strong to wash away my sins.

Don't worry. I will always reserve the table for old time's sake. This time around it will be different, for I will see you not and hear you not.

The time came for you to go home, but I have just been robbed of ever again leaning and tapping you on the shoulder for that big ole laugh. The price I would pay to see those mischievous eyes of yours flicker once more with golden wonder. Tonight it will be a moment of silence; today it will be the rebirth of our friendship, I will set aside my schedule for you, for tonight it is just you and me and the eternal bond we are going to forge.

Fear not, for I am not going to cross the river to the other side or do something foolish. Oh no, no. Tonight is reserved for you, my dear friend, for I want to know the address to the other side where you live. Is the grass always green? Do you see the end of the rainbow? And do the birds chip early in the morning? Too many questions to answer for one man. Come, my friend, for the fallen heroes wait for us to come to supper.

Fight Cancer!

What a loss for society, yet another victory for the C word, 'cause every hill it climbs, it rolls down with another curve ball. It comes in different forms, like the devil in the blue dress, for it alone is captivating to that skin. As the couture gently caresses his throat, I hope the tightness of it does not squeeze the air out of his lungs and make his ovaries shift while his pancreas screams free from congestion.

Although you may have a long journey ahead of you—and you feel like all is lost and the energy is completely sucked out of you, and the roads look long and windy—take refuge, but this time alone. Break out of your comfort zone, 'cause it's just the beginning of the battle, and you have something to prove.

Don't bend backward for cancer. Put on your boxing gloves and get into the ring. See and hear only the chanting of the people. Focus only on the support of your loved ones. And wiggle your toes, for you've got a lot of stepping to do. Don't feel like you lost to the invincible parasite because you cannot do the things you used to do. Instead, focus on your focus. Hold a hand if you feel let down; talk to others going through the same fight as you. Along the way, you had better equipped yourself and solidified your armor. Don't hesitate to cry when you need to; then again, do not let it consume you, for you're not a weakling, and you do not give up easily.

You do not have to wear the wig, but that decision should come from you, for your strength is in numbers. And, yes, you can still stand up for yourself. Look into the mirror and smile, for being bald is beautiful. We recognize your fight and salute you.

The Neighbor's Dog

The neighbor has one of the sweetest dogs in the world, but the loudest on the block.

I refuse to let that dog rule me like the others who lived here before me. That thing will lick you to death and then kiss your ears off your head and send smiles to your lips. Sure thing, it is a brat, but I dare not complain, because it keeps everyone company but me. It growls at everything from a dancing shadow to a nut-eating squirrel. Maybe it needs more friends. *Ah non?* Who would have thought of that? *Mais le chien est fort chez lui.*

Today I decided to meet my friend, the dog. It was exciting finally to come face to face with the loud keeper, the squirrel chaser, and the ghost hunter. More than anything, it was kinda hard to pick out an outfit. Maybe I was trying to have it like me and not bark at the scent of my perfume. I must admit that collar around its neck looked like a pissed-off stopwatch. Today I shall try to think happy thoughts, for *ma maison est plein de peuple aujourdhui, et je suis très fier.*

The table looks set for a conqueror, but my watery plate of steak had my friend waving a peace flag. *Y and depuis quand mon ami?* Slowly I looked its way and could swear it had a smirk on its face. I refuse the peace treaty! Somebody escort this cold stranger out, for he is a wrapped-up, shaggy hell infuser with a twist of lemon and a brandy waiting to be ignited.

Oh wait! *Excuse moi, mon ami.* Sometimes I get intense when ordering a brandy with ice and hope you do accept my sincere apology. For to think twice about it would have me believe you are a drunken dog on a watch and no better to your owner, huh? Come, come, I can certainly treat you to a delicious prize I am holding. What did say you? To deny such an invitation would be to … Do I hear a *woof, woof?* Good, good. Now this is a peace treaty to accept, for I will always remember to love to love you.

Sleeping with the Enemy

The mistake was mine to have met you. I had forgotten to call you, but you insisted on meeting. The hangover was terrible, but the day was beautiful. How could I have said no? The sky was so bright; the sun smiled down on earth, looking just in the right direction. Clouds were parted, and the heavens looked down with a wild interest, as if having first-class tickets in a movie theater.

While I drove to you, wondering what was in store, my stomach churned. My eyes were still in recovery from the night before. I longed for a cold wet drink, but I wanted a quick shot to you, so away I drove onto the two-way lane to meet you.

I should have known it was a disaster from the beginning. The narrow road leading to your house was so tiny, it was like something out of this world. And my old clunker wasn't helping either. I had to reverse but was scared to end up in the pond right behind me. I took off my seat belt in case the worst was to happen. I had to park and open the door just a little bit. Yes, it was my emergency exit, a dash to safety. I had to take care of me when I looked ahead. A head was what I should have had, the smarts to turn back and drive home. But then I would have missed my sweet mistake, one less experience lost and less the wiser.

You played a game, because you have been played in the past. You helped just a little to see me wither. When I figured you out, you made excuses to buy my excitement, 'cause you were indeed bored. Only the Lord knows if it was just of yourself or of others around you.

I was sleeping with the enemy, bored with the wings of hell, tortured by the restless immortality of those refuse-to-be-forgotten souls. His heart is made of cement, but once shattered, it turns to little specks of dangerous glass. No, no, no heart—just a hole. Sinkable? I dare not answer, for his name is not engraved on my finger nor a precious paper stored away in the precious little box tugging away on my heartstring. That cross is not mine to bear. Oh no!

Please let me make my sweet mistake, for I have to go and I have to leave. Good-byes were not meant for me nor was sharing your bed, clothed in a white robe. For I am not empty inside, chasing a delusional feeling. I told you the heavens heard my cry, and your mood changed—I would almost say to jealousy, for you burned with envy. Good thing you were already in my rear-view mirror as I drove past you.

My French Girl

The way you speak, the way you walk, and most of all your accent drive me crazy.

I have not yet made you mine, but can you be mine? I hear you like wine; so do I. Would you like foreign cuisine to please your taste buds or being swept off your feet for breakfast in Paris, lunch in Rome, and dinner in Japan? I am by no means tired nor am I a player, even though I have been called the eligible bachelor numerous times.

I would like to make you mine, so tell me, are you taken? Would you want to travel the world with me? It's definitely well cut out and will fit you, if you like excitement as I do. Private jets, boats, and a whole island—just you and me having fun with no care in the world. I can teach you things you've only heard of, and I can make you melt like a bar of chocolate.

You pique my interest. When I listen to a conversation, I hope your name is mentioned, for then I am complete. Don't worry about what they think, do, or say, for I care about just what I see in you. You are my most delicate flower, and when I happen to catch a glimpse of your smile, I wish to be lost in your embrace. Come, be my Juliet, with only the happy ending.

Do you love kids? If so we can volunteer together, for it keeps me one step closer to being a really good father. Only by practicing can I perfect my skills. What kind of roses do you like? I can order a room full for you, if you don't mind. I am not obsessed; I am a man in love. I hope you can decipher the difference, because rejection hurts like a bad cold.

Memories

Some would say it was built to last and to be treasured forever. Others argue and beg for a different opinion. Regardless of the circumstances, memories are what make you and me different from the rest. It may be cherished or rejected because of the experiences we may have encountered. This is indeed what makes the outcome of life so outstanding.

The memories of yesterday may help us toward predicting the future. They may guide and shape us or just plain help us in the circumstances we went through. Memories are our best friends, for love was never wavering; they stood by us when those around us doubted. They polished the tears at midnight and brought a smile when those roses fell. They were never jealous, just hopeful, for they had tremendous faith in whatever chapter we turned to.

When the doubts came, memories brought up our painful past to strengthen us and our happy memories to make us laugh, for they longed to see us create a happy chapter. Memories are never gone. They are just stored, because to forget would be to forget yourself and to deny would be to weaken your bond.

You may chose not to speak of memories, for you are not a storyteller. You may choose not to bring them up, because you look forward to life this time around. You may expect the unexpected, but this time you—yes, you—are ready for whatever comes your way. For you have been educated by the teachers of old. Your skin has been forged from a belly of the steel and passed through a hell house. You have broken the once unbroken chain, with every doubts banished from your thoughts.

Yesterday's thoughts are incognito, but if you look to the sun for new inspirations and your memories for guidance, somewhere beneath that ocean of love and flooded banks is a shadow that lies thankful for the memories.

The People Around You

The people around you—do not trust them, because when they smile, you never know their intentions. Be polite, smile back, for the world would be a heck of a boring place with no bright, chipped, brown, coffee-stained, gummy-bear, pearly white, bleached-toothed smile.

They may like you, yes, and it's okay to like them back. But never go to sleep with your eyes closed, for then alone they come with daggers at night. They are no Santa Clauses, but they will come down the chimney. They are jealous, but you already knew that, for words have been spat around, and the gossips aired out laundry hot out of a dryer. They envy you, from everything you do to everything you wear. For they are too lazy to hustle and bustle like you did to get to where you are.

My friend, that is just the tip of an iceberg. Those you call friends should be called associates, for they are likely to spit fire in your right eye while tending to the left one. They are the nurse on duty when the doctor asks for a sick day. They will run you over and then call for an ambulance. They thrive on their dirty spats and feast on their crumbs.

They will try to come for what you have. Be prepared to stand up and make them see that they have just crossed the dirty waters. Like those who toil hard for success, you have marked your territory whether you are young money, old money, or still trying to make it into the game.

If you have courage to pursue it, swim with the whales and dine with the sharks. Then you can certainly forge your empire and build on solid ground. For when they come, they won't meet you at the Alps; you will meet them at their door. Be keen. Be a good listener, the last to talk. Weigh your opponent, for if he is full of gibberish, match him with his own talk. He will definitely call you idiotic. Smile and be polite. That doesn't mean you are a fool, for you have just had the upper hand; you knew how to examine and classify that particular scenario.

The people around you will have plenty of ways they see you; they know how they want you to be, to react, and to live. Remember to always let them, for they feed off their game. Denying them a fish will make them hunger for sushi. Be different, be bold, be courageous while always paying tribute to the whales.

Patience

P atience is known for the energy you must gather, let alone the time-consuming meditation you have to go through to keep biting your tongue. I refuse to let my anger rule my patience. For days like these, I seek the Holy Ghost, for he must have gone far ahead of me; he must have taken the morning train. Why does he depart when I am the body he needs so he can see the world in another version? Maybe the vision he sees makes him long for the one he misses. Either way, I am hopping on that night train to catch him by sunrise.

You may say I can pray for an angel. Yes, that thought has crossed my mind a dozen times, but truth be told, it is very complicated, for things are not as simple as they read. I must agree on the fact that another strange angel would be nice and exciting, but the old one knows me. Another ghost may sound seducing, but my body craves the usual.

I long to meet him again and ask if he can make me whole, for the hope in me is too strong. Thus I pray that I, I will not be rotten when I reach the finish line, for the morning showers feel good, thoughts of ripe strawberries linger in my mouth, and the sweet scent of an intoxicating aroma lingers in the air.

Most of all, I hope my patience will make me new, for I long for the new. This cross-eyed vision is rendering my sense senseless. For a ghost of harmony we were bound and with true colors we enjoyed the pattern of the world, for it is giant enough for two. Yet it is complicated enough for one person to understand and gentle enough to explore through the vision of a sleeping beauty.

I'd rather be awake and enjoy all the scenery, for it comes at too dear a price to be sold. It cannot be bought, I say, but it can be savored and devoured. A hungry tummy it will gladly feed.

As I look out, I see the traveling train kissing the morning fog as its tail disappears into what appears to be a gleam of morning light. I am glad I was wide awake to enjoy this moment, for this reunion has been long talked of, this meeting is finally here, and my toes are all curled up in anticipation.

To My Grandmother, Princess Elizabeth

I miss your smile, your laughter, and your kindness. The twinkle in your eye shone with hope, and how much you believed in me. You taught me well, and you taught me right. You gently corrected when I misstepped, for our souls were old and entwined like the stars in heaven. You opened my eyes when I trusted too much, for you saw beyond me the path of men who were truly conniving as they strode from every walk of life. You were truly a princess in every sense, for you were gentle with your touch. With your warmth in your gentle opinions, you fed your people without any questions asked.

You, the white woman, were adored by your people and beloved by your family. You were the epitome of class, for you did not wait to be given anything. You believed that hard work, dedication, and perseverance pay off. Yes, you strode far from home but always looked back into the society where you came about.

Not once did you desert your people or be gone for too long. You gave up your happy days, just to make sure I was okay. You sang when I cried, held my hands when I laughed, and strongly stood behind me at all times.

I hope I have not failed you, for I returned like you wanted. But this peace is hard to keep. You asked of me something so small yet so big. I will try, for I love you. I will put the pieces together, for I still care. I will glue it, for I believe in a tomorrow with no arguing. I want to make you smile wherever you are, for together we can be strong.

Gone but still here is the warmth in your eyes, the glow in your cheeks, and the promise in your embrace. These will surely keep me from stepping aside. Sometimes I feel like giving up, for how can I be the one burdened with this burden? I ran far away from this task, yet you gently sailed me back. I rebelled and cast away what I had known, but you gently smiled and picked up the pieces. I begged you to choose someone else, but you saw something in me. When I doubted, you tried to map out the puzzle so I could better understand my full potential. When I tried to shift the wind and caught a glimpse of your face, I felt your sad breeze.

I have accepted the call, for I drank from the cup to quench my thirst. And just like the candle that still burns between us, your presence is ever strong. Your memory and my memory shall forever float in clouds of memories, and our names will forever remain entwined.

Yours truly, your beloved and devoted grandchild.

Fallen Angel

You cry, he ain't perfect!
Are you?
Condemn him!
Why? Is it because you are doomed?
Crucify him!
Don't you see he already carries the cross?
He ain't fit to be among us!
Who are you to decide on such a matter?
His tongue has been cursed!
Here let me rinse yours.
This is blasphemy!
Says who?
He speaks like he knows the ways of the old!
At least he banks on what he knows.
What? What? How dare you speak when I speak?
Forgive me, for I thought you were done.

Nay, nay! Listen here, lad. I don't know who you think you are, but that man has no place at the tables of the mortals. He belongs where the belly of hell rolls thunders, the devils pick on their skin, and the scorching flames from the bottomless pit of hell rise in the belly of the traitor to let him know of pain he will never forget.

Forgive me, but have you been to hell or better yet driven through its gates? Or do these thoughts you think of arise when you find fault in another mortal you don't like?

Who are you to question me when I speak of nothing but the truth?

I indeed. You give the poor man no room for justifications.

Justifications!

Who said that was an option? With all due respect, if you were to trade in the shoes of the lad, would you rather someone help you tie your shoestrings or choke you with them?

Why would my shoestrings be undone in the first place?

Ah! Forgive me, Sire. You see, your shoestrings would be undone the night before, so before you slip your shoes back on, before catching the glimpse of the first morning light, they will need to be tied once more. Yesterday is gone; today is a brand-new day. The lad deserves a chance to chance his way out.

Blasphemy! Blasphemy! You side with the traitor.

Very well, you say he is a fallen angel and now a mortal, aye?

Yes, yes, very so indeed.

Would you say you are a product of the first humans that walked the earth, sire?

Eh, lad, are you referring to me as one of the fallen angels too? You must have slept on the wrong side of me bed.

Ha, ha, ha! That's very convenient for you to say when the odds pile up. Now, is that a mere coincidence, or do I need to change pillows for my naps?

Why would you find that thing over there worth supporting?

For the same reason you have no proof of having visited hell.

That is a new story on its own. For when I passed through hell, you were busy saving men not worth saving.

Ah, I see. Why would I want to ruin your midday with such an unwavering thought of mine, when I can bury the hatchet and find a tree to chop. But nay, nay, truth be told, trees will grow, their leaves will blossom, and they will bear fruits. And when they are ripe for the picking, we will sink our teeth deep down and taste the nectar of that first fresh bite as if we just conquered a whole Persian army. That taste, my friend, is a taste of invading and taking what is not ours, for the tree never gave you permission for the plucking. And when the ripe fruits fall unto the ground, it still does not tell you to bear his cross. But you cannot resist invading a territory that is not yours, and thereby you shall always reap what you sow. Now let the fallen angel speak for him, and only he alone knows the way to once again rise.

All-American Rejects

Cold shoulders and stares so long it sends chills down my spine. Disregard what they think, 'cause thinking was meant for food for thought. Feed my brain, for it is going senseless and is in need of air to breathe. The ifs and buts are not terms associated with my programmed vocabulary. Please, I pray you, understand that I hate nonsense, and do take out the thrash per the request of my design every evening. Recycle first, and the regular comes next, for my system needs room to reboot.

My disk may be a little rusty. Damn that engineer and his long-acquired education for failing on my parts, for I am parting this on my own. Hold on. I need to find close quarters, for the wind is on my back so strong the force pushes me two steps forward. My balance I catch, and I curse at this windy weather, for the clouds whisper a different song. I sing to me to console the wicked tunes. Thriflent is my bow of defense; gently I can go your way. I must come to terms, for this tune you demand with demands too much to bear.

Why whisper American rejections when the only ejected sense here is mine? The crowded space and loud, strange sounds come your way, and empty stares bellow strange requests. This tune is killing me to keep it, for the American reject speaks of tunes so diverse, for many a man walks that part of life. The conditions are clear, for clarifications come when no man stands the test of time. I refuse to let the shadows rise before your face and thus corrupt your sensibility, for that innocence must be left behind. A new man should be formed.

A thought, I thought, and a way of life may be denied to you once too often. Corrupted dreams of the one on top—stingy, he wants it all; he wants all to himself. The people come to terms with it, for if they object, they are subjected to the language of the silent man. He comes in many ways: control, deceit, greed, anger, confused happiness, stormy dreams. Corruption comes in whatever sense it may be put when he wakes. He likes to see himself differently in the mirror, for the mere feeling of not dining from a round bowl makes him the master. Master of what? American rejects?

Hahaha, so he was once an American reject? Good to know. He does not feel like he belongs to the clan of the rejected. Is it because he is a clam that has been chowed down on already?

A reject just graduated with a different stripe on his shoulder, for his ego matches the banner he upholds. One is a sad tale to follow. Horrific are the ways painted. The color he chooses ease his senses. Dare not paint strange, for he will refuse you a check. Welcome, welcome, welcome! Grab a quick visa or win a lottery. Join the line, for we are the All-American rejects with a twist of chance.

Unanswered Questions

Are there times you feel like you are divided between the heavens and the earth?

How did you come to be?

Who were my great-great-great-great-great-great-great-great-great-great-great-great-grandparents?

What did they look like?

Is there a God?

Should I really follow the religion I know, or should I choose another one?

Am I nondenominational?

Should I strive to be like my parents or adventure on my own?

What would the world be like if everyone spoke the same language and we were all one race?

Are we going to be racing to the finish line?

Is there going to be some sort of judgment day?

Is my religion better than the others?

Should I strive for perfection, even though perfection seems like being too perfect?

Does the good I do for others help them in any ways?

Why is there so much violence and segregation—so much of a black-and-white issue, when I am in the middle of the road?

Why is there so much violence and segregation?

Is my love ever good enough?

Why do families forsake their loved ones in the name of greed, anger, jealousy, and betrayal?

If I dream tonight, can I wake up to a better tomorrow?

Why is the revenge of men as desperate and low as their ego?

Why do I love you when I know someday it might hurt?

If love is as blind as a bat, what do you call the desperate cries of an infant?

Why do two blind decide for a date out of town?

My questions are unanswered. The truth I seek is within me, for I listen to my instincts. It bears the cross of salvation; it lectures my thoughts and feeds my body, even though I find fault in the world. I stand not alone, for numerous others stand alongside me and question the questions and dare others to question, for they are afraid to question these questions because they hate to feel like the outcast. Let me be the outcast and question these questions.

Wolf in Sheep Clothing

It ain't like you like me, but pretend you do 'cause faking come easy. Lying rolls off your tongue like icing on a cake. Care you, dare say you, for you will leave me in the cold and abandon the thought that we had ever crossed paths. Let me wrap myself with my lonely cloak 'cause at least I am not bothered by the thoughts of your wild ways. Your path is not the path I want to go down at the moment. We have two different destinies, but that does not mean I hate you to come a life-time. Stab me in the back, then ask me to go to an emergency room. For many men you made take such a visit. Your smile is the spit of a venomous snake, and I refuse to let it gently travel and consume me. I will cut out the bitten area and let it bleed. As I watch it bleed, so will the time I spent with you pass.

How deep were your conniving thoughts. How fast did they travel?

Good thing I came prepared, for in no man do I fully trust. *Trust* a five-letter word, but it's hard to find individuals to live up to it. I swear it is the brother of integrity, for hand in hand they travel, and if you have one and not the other, you are not a just man. Just men in these day and this age? Ice fishing in the middle of June will give you more chances of catching a glimpse of the rainbow and hopefully the munchkin guarding the doors. I had my suspicions, but the benefit of doubt I gave you. Now the mirror I look unto reflects none other than blurry images of soft butterflies, for hopefully it is still in the moth stage.

I wonder what my next transformation will be. I dare not tell anyone, for my left hand envies my right, depending on the time of day. My trust you broke; my loyalty you trampled on. Be gone, and let the wind erase your footsteps every inch of the way, for the cry I cry is none other than a just cry.

The Silent Mailman

Bound by the contract or bound by the lack of your tongue, your friendly wave, the sweet smile, and the exact response when I say good morning. I hate this thought, for I want to strike up a conversation with the blue man—yes, the one carrying the mail. I want to tell him how sometimes I love the smell of freshly cut grass or how the leaves change color with every season or how I miss seeing the morning light when I wake up a tad too late. I want to tell him how I wait impatiently for him at my windowsill, be it in the freezing winter or the scorching summer sun. Sometimes I would like to tell him I am his number-one fan when he arrives early with that work check I have been waiting on. I would also like to thank him for how he sorts my mail. For he truly cares for a second; for him it means a second less junk. Yet a sweet smile is all I know to expect of him.

I see that van of his drive through the neighborhood, and I wonder how far he traveled to come to see me today. I like to look forward and think there are days he will say something. I wonder, will his van ever break down and will he ask for help? I like to think so. Then maybe I will get a chance to open him up a little.

Nay, nay, nay. All these days gone by and all these years have gone silent, for silence seems to be becoming the norm around here. I want a different day and different expectation, for I know many a man strides along to the same questions, but too many fear to ask or to voice the feeling. Some just conform to the usual while the others just go with the flow.

Sharp Ones

The last dream came around, and I saw you alive in it. I wonder why the draining thoughts warm me, for the pleasant ones still come when I think of you. I lay down the fighting elements, for they wear me down and tear us down. We love the happy times and stay apart when they are not. I love the way you see the bright future and take the time to listen to the sweet melancholy of my voice. This tells me you adore every note I hit, for every pitch seems a perfect balance with the attitude of right now. The driving force of your love drives the motor in my engine. It runs not on gas or fuel, but on the energy of the sharp one.

I dare challenge myself to let go, let loose, and love you. I dare too many things but, darling, I dare to say I dare not, for he who is sharp dares no dare. Even the ocean never knows when it may run dry. I lean on the rocks, for they are well forged. Your opinion I seek when I need a chime, but the decision is mine to bear and one I must make. I trust me to not let me down. I trust you to be you, for I dare not ask of you a disappointment. I don't want you to swear by the rivers that our ancestors drank from or the fire experimented with by our forefathers or the womb that bears fruits for a beautiful life on earth. As a sharp one, I don't want to make my other blade dull. I will let you take your stride, and if our paths happen to cross again, I will make sure I am sharp enough to see my own reflection. For the image changes over time, but the wits, if well planted, yield abundantly.

I promise to try to keep the promise of the possibility of being open to the roads you tread. I can't follow, for I will trample on your footprints, but I will fly above and keep watch. I want to see from the vantage point of the bird and greet the eagles. Let me get lost in the clouds and find refuge if it does not rain, for the sky is clear and so are my dreams.

I want to soar and let go, for I will catch my strength as I look straight at that image still left to be seen. For it is the only way I can come to terms with my demons. The slow impact of the curse alone makes hell roar in fury, let alone spit out molten fire, leaving with it a cold, harsh reality of a dark realm.

I know it is the battle from within that sends hatred down a sultry spine, for mine carries weight and cannot be examined. It is not crooked for the curious, and thus far from the holy. Middle of the road, I posted, but I did take turns to stare at the shattered glass. I have a pain like no other. I heal slowly and memorably, for 'tis with every healing stroke I remember the past and mistakes far too great to mold, shape, reconstruct, revamp, and forever revive.

Random Thoughts of a Teenage Girl

I hate my new school, but I like my friends. This movie is so cool, and I wish I had enough money to shop till I drop at the mall. I wonder who will be elected homecoming queen this year—not like I care, but I still care to know. I like candies and anything sweet. Speaking of sweet, the new guy who is sweet happens to be a high school sweetheart, and all the girls are crushing on him so hard.

Eww, this sweet in my mouth just got sour. Whatever! I want to paint my nails red, not that my parents will let me. They just ruined my life, and I don't know if I will be asked to go to prom. Everyone will be there, and hopefully the guy who asks me to go is cute. Why do I look fat in this dress? I swear this mirror is seeing things and showing me wrong images. I have to go on a diet—no more calories. But I love Amanda's cupcakes. That girl wants me fat!

Tomorrow I am going to see a movie with the girls. They are all going to be wearing cute little outfits. Okay, I know, I know, I'm not going. Something came up, right?

It does all the time.

I am going to my room. I don't want to talk to anyone, and I hate boys! My life is ruined until I lose more weight. I'm going to use my mom's workout machines. It would be so cool to have all my friends live with me. I would be the happiest person on earth, and we could all eat cotton candy and watch those scary movies I get scared of watching alone. We could set up a camp-like place in the backyard and count how many new stars were born today. They will cheat because they will count the same stars twice in a row. It will be the best sleep ever in a long time, and we will talk about everything that happens at school, listen to the coolest songs, make our own decisions, and buy tickets to go see our favorite artist perform.

Speaking of making my own decisions, I would love to change the menu in the school cafeteria. The food sucks, and my lunch is not helping it either. My teachers are okay, but they sure know how to bombard us with homework. Yeah, the principal is cool too.

Next spring I hope to join the girls soccer team, but while waiting for that, I wish teenagers could book a flight to Mars. Who am I kidding, right? These are just the random thoughts of a teenage girl.

A Good Mother's Wish

This is a wish upon the stars, the ones that never die, the hope that shines through, the unbroken veil that lingers as you grow. The warm affection comes padded with a kiss. The laughter brings about home-cooked dinners, the loud sound of the crock pot on the stove, and the yelling from the kitchen. These tell you Mom is home. Her eyes shine with love, and her thoughts are sweet. She sometimes holds tight and forgets to let go.

I am grown; my footsteps will follow her veil. Her wish will make me want to reach for the sky, for I hear it is the limit. Her wishes are numerous, but they all mean well. If they were placed in order, it would make me reflect before I walked. But none other speaks of loving, dear, and remains faithfully unmoved through the centuries.

A dove represents the purity of the divine love we share. In a beating heart we were bound before my arrival. My flesh was made whole by her body, and the whole deserves to give her thanks. I am out of the nine-month process, but her process just began. She looks to my whole being as if contemplating what she could have done better. A better person she hopes for; a braver being she prays for; a great guide she asks for; and a good heart she hopes I borrowed along the way. For perfect in her book is what she sees when she looks at me. And if the other coin says otherwise, she is sure to flip it again to remain positive.

Disappoint her not, for the wait might make her weary. I pray she sets her alarm clock. School her I dare not, for she is the epitome of class itself. I kneel to drink from that well of purity. Her beauty alone makes me know she dined with the Greek goddess of Rome in an era set forth with many things to come.

Today is the new, and I look to her guidance, her generosity. Thus she forges the strength in me that arises in numbers. I pledge such a pledge that a good mother's wish does not go wasted. For I stand a man to challenge me to my limits. The test put forth can my bond uphold her worthy tears, for I will pave the path she began and water the rivers she worshiped, for I stand to make that wish hold.

Ten Thousand Milestone

Maybe it is the thought of departing that makes us cry. Or are we afraid of the unknown once that destination is right in front of us? The slow good-byes are long, for the one thing we are absolutely sure about is that the love we share for one another will be gone for a while—maybe a long, long, very long while. The cherished times will remain engraved in my brain, for that cannot be erased. The distance will be a huge factor, no doubt. But look to the stars, and count the opposite direction and then two forward, one row back, left-hand corner in the center, right where the opposite ends merge. There I will be, right in front of you.

I don't know if I will have the luxury of a delivery service, but I would hate to miss him. Keep the faith of one day reuniting, for I tremble at the thought of your pale ghost. The flames burn, but they burn anew. The lonely roads crossed will make me ten thousand miles away from you, and it does no justice to linger on that thought. I pray the roads back to you will be straight and forward, for broken bridges are hard to mend, and I'd hate to catch a cold while doing just that. Forever, you say. What keeps you busy while I journey to the unknown? For I know the river is fresh, the catch is easy, winter is a ways away, and I hate to admit I am jealous of your surroundings: familiar faces, the restaurants that make the most delicious meals. I dismiss this thought but will fancy to play a game of chess with you if your river of tears can stop flowing, for I've got an hour to last me a while.

Bring a Scrabble board. Let's scribble this word of parting ways together, for I long to hit the triple mark and make you smile.

Deny me not the look of lost love, for it brings the morning glory of tingle on your skin and sends the blush of winds on your cheeks. Let me check, for this is only to check my letters, not that I do not love to see the time together. I hate to hear you read out every second, for those make me the lonely traveler. For some reason, it makes me feel like I came underprepared. But I know we can come together as one and put one that makes a meaning, while refining the just cause for this journey will ever make me closer to you, and it will double your score for a chance of a lifetime together.

Slow Good-byes

The shadows are wide-awake, for the constant riot of the soul forces the body to come awake. I will come again when the wake is near and sleep when the hunt is over. I dream. The dream is big; no little dream goes unnoticed except you let it slide. Call on your senses when your mind goes dry, for the waterfall never runs dry. The pit burns the fire you needed, but the height it attains might scare you, for the near is far away. When you look at the burning log, it tells you of a quick glimpse of passion— one forged by you very own hands. You understand the foreign language spoken with the eyes, because your lips have kissed a tongue far too warm.

The nights bellow for you to come to sleep, but the morning refuses to let your eyes close. The pacing back and forth only drives your energy to another hemisphere. You dare to try to reach it, for you have powers played by the nights. Round and round, you find what you left behind, for your own thoughts have been well put your energy can be giving by forces unknown. You will put it to good use, you say.

Alone you wonder for the next. Your anticipation has led you to think you might have been bestowed blessings by the angels, for they alone sing with no mistakes. But you are far from joining the realm, for the golden crown you wear comes in different shades. They will harvest the fruit you have so patiently planted and happily watered, for you have spoken the language of the eyes and let your face come into contact with your self. You whispered a song so sweet and caused your tongue to seek a million languages hidden in the journey of your greetings. None is too small, for every might put together to speak and seduce. Your senses will definitely travel to your brain, for it alone can unleash the heat from the pupils and calm the weary eyes for a second look. Look with love every time you face the fact, because the whole you made it refined. When you do see the glorious days, think of the many spheres your eyes have decode to bring you this far. Rest your weary eyes, 'cause they cause the journey too long to be wide shut.

Sinking Man

The rivers may be cold, my feet too numb to move, my lips blue with hope for rescue. My hands, freezing with no doubts, tell me I am on my own, for my flesh is wearing thin with every slap of the current on my senses. I pray to be delivered from this rapture, but then again I seek the people of the ocean. None will rescue me or my senses from the slow rise of the evening wave. None will rescue me, because I speak a different language unknown to them. The water can't translate, for they are hungry for the feed. The shark speaks of terror, and my sole wish is to have a life jacket of courage.

Away, away, I float. The salty taste of the ocean breaks my lips with every taste.

I am dehydrated from the taste, and my eyes cry red rivers. My head holds and holds for hope; my legs remain to be questioned. The tide has risen too high, and my neck is breaking from glancing around my environment. Sleep is long gone, for if I sleep, sleep deep I will.

Let me resurrect with a wave slapping my ear, for it alone knows my lonely struggle. The ocean is not my best friend, though it hangs from the bosom like we were joined at the hips at the time of birth. The hold is so strong, it is crippling my senses. The more I beg for release, the more it intrudes with every touch, sound, and taste of its salty belief.

This raft is too strong and high as I get tossed with every aggressive motion. It loves the rough play, for I tire, punished to such limits. But it plays like a newborn with a fragile brain. It smiles with innocence. I am sinking, and it still smiles and claps. Please clap no more till you mature enough to understand the path of the grown and the struggle of a sinking man.

Forget about the quarrel, for the ocean is still not my best friend, for it is too wide to please. I reject friendship with its piranha friends, for they will eat while I sleep and invite me to lunch when awake.

My only comfort is to comfort myself, and this headache needs another body, for I am too tired to carry its troubles, too tired to feel a thing. My arms are stretched wide, for I refuse to sink. Together I can become one with the wave. For once I will let it guide my back and will pray the dolphins take me safely to shore.

Friendship

Who are you kidding? Friendship is scarce, and most likely two shadows befriend you. The wind whispers of envy; it carries the message like fresh pollen on a beautiful spring morning. Your friend you befriended is the shadow you may never know, for you long to know him, and you want him to know him. Thus trust in your heart is a hole. Forget what you think you might know, for the one you know may be the one to bring you far into questioning your own being.

You never have a best hand, for you never know just when he might betray you. Few men have had the good luck of coming out with both hands clean. For rare is the man who speaks with a clean voice and wishes to see you do well, for his heart aches as he lays his body to rest. Then the evil creeps up on him. The magnificent thoughts of the days will be long gone, replaced by the surgery of the wild and wicked ones. If you are not too careful, he will drink and dance with the devil as if to celebrate your birthday. Such is the wavering of friendship. He can't be happy with your success 24/7, for if you thought such a thought, you might need a Galileo telescope. Gone is his flesh but refined was his once-invented vision of a genuine masterpiece. He will be honored if you borrowed it for a day.

The checklist is long indeed, making it what separates the two. But the midway thoughts may give it an added boost for booze with an open eye. Time may never know till you test it, for it alone will weed out rotten spells and help you brush off the dust from your balcony. Don't bother if it remains too clean, for it will always get tainted spots somewhere along the line.

Friendship is nice, but never forget your lonely times, for loneliness gives you timely moments to reflect upon yourself. Be first to please, for no other does it better than you. Lead yourself away from gossips, for only fools entertain the nonsense of a fallen comrade. May your wits be quickly to play, your fingers slow to harm, and your lips careful as you respond. For a wise man you strive to be; know that respect comes once it is extended. Make a sound judgment when you choose a better friend for tomorrow. If you have a friend you traveled a milestone with, count your lucky stars up in the sky, for they know that with friendship comes coordination.